OFFICE OF
**INSPECTOR GENERAL**
U.S. DEPARTMENT OF THE INTERIOR

I0428091

# GUAM PUBLIC SAFETY

## OFFICE OF
# INSPECTOR GENERAL
### U.S.DEPARTMENT OF THE INTERIOR

NOV 2 0 2012

The Honorable Eddie Baza Calvo
Governor of Guam
Ricardo J. Bordallo Governor's Complex
Adelup, Guam 96910

Subject:    Final Evaluation Report – Guam Public Safety
           Report No. HI-EV-GUA-0002-2011

Dear Governor Calvo:

This report contains the results of our evaluation of Guam Public Safety. We reviewed the ability of Guam's Police Department (GPD), Fire Department (GFD), and Homeland Security (GHS) to meet the current public safety needs of Guam's citizens and prepare for the increase in population resulting from the military buildup.   We determined that despite efforts made by the public safety agencies, GFD and GPD are unable to meet the current needs of Guam and will be unable to meet the needs of the anticipated increase in population. Unless shortcomings in staffing, infrastructure, vehicles, maintenance, and training are addressed, the citizens of Guam will continue to be at risk. GHS, which is 100 percent Federally funded, meets Guam's current needs, but as Federal funding decreases, it may be unable to maintain its current level of service without local funding.

We offered three recommendations to which we requested your response. We appreciate your response to the draft report (appendix 4) on August 26, 2012. Based on your response, we consider the three recommendations unresolved (appendix 5). As the U.S. Department of the Interior's conduit for coordinating Federal policy and activities with insular area territories and government, the Office of Insular Affairs (OIA) monitors and tracks Guam's governance efforts, which would include resolution and implementation of the recommendations contained in the attached report. Accordingly, we have requested that OIA track Guam's progress in implementing and resolving these recommendations. The legislation creating the Office of Inspector General requires that we report to Congress semiannually on all audit reports issued, actions taken to implement our recommendations, and recommendations that have not been implemented.

If you have any questions concerning this letter or the subject report, please contact Mr. Michael P. Colombo, Regional Manager, at 916-978-5653.

Sincerely,

Mary L. Kendall
Deputy Inspector General

# Table of Contents

# Results in Brief

The protection from and prevention of events endangering the public's safety, such as crime and natural and manmade disasters, is a vital function of any government. Guam faces increased challenges in meeting the current public safety needs of the citizens, as well as the needs associated with the impending military buildup. We examined the ability of Guam's Police Department (GPD), Fire Department (GFD), and Homeland Security (GHS) to meet the safety and response needs of Guam's citizens and prepare for the increase in population.

GFD and GPD cannot meet the current public safety needs of Guam and will not meet the needs of the anticipated increase in population from the military buildup. Unless the Government of Guam (GovGuam) addresses shortcomings in staffing, infrastructure, vehicles, maintenance, and training, the citizens of Guam will continue to be at risk from events that could endanger public safety. While GHS, which is 100 percent federally funded, is able to meet Guam's current needs, as Federal funds decrease, it may be unable to maintain its current level of service without local funding.

Many of the weaknesses we found result from inadequate planning and funding from GovGuam. Specifically, GovGuam has been reactive in funding the agencies' needs, such as staffing, vehicles, and maintenance. It also has heavily relied on Federal funding for many of the agencies' operational needs. To better address public safety concerns, GPD, GFD, and GHS should compare the current level of service to the desired level of service and reconcile any differences through planning, budgeting, and monitoring activities.

# Introduction

## Objective

We examined the extent that the Guam Police Department (GPD), Guam Fire Department (GFD), and Guam Homeland Security (GHS) are able to meet the safety needs of the citizens of Guam and prepare for the increase in population due to military buildup. We reviewed existing programs, infrastructure, equipment, emergency preparedness, resources, and training.

## Background

GPD, GFD, and GHS safeguard those who live, work, and visit Guam. Each agency's mission statement reflects its purpose. For example, GPD's mission is to protect life and property, prevent crime, enforce the laws, and maintain order. GFD's mission statement is to provide quality emergency and non-emergency fire and emergency medical services. GHS's mission is to coordinate and facilitate all GovGuam, military, and Federal liaison response agencies and their resources in mitigating, preparing, responding, and recovering from any and all types of emergencies to protect the lives, environment, and property of Guam.

In 2011, Guam's population, including the military, was approximately 180,000. Due to the potential military buildup, Guam's population may increase with the relocation of Marines and their dependents and support services to the island. Previous planning efforts, based on the relocation of 8,600 Marines, projected an increase of 80,000 people in Guam. The projected increase of 80,000 people includes not only the Marines, but their families, construction workers, and other jobs that arise with a population increase. The exact impact on Guam's population is unknown. Recent developments, however, indicate that the number of relocating troops may be closer to 4,500. Population growth and the associated shift in demographics, traffic patterns, and land use (e.g., new commercial development, and higher-density housing) could pose significant challenges for law enforcement and emergency preparedness.

### Service Expectations and Personnel

GPD has 372 employees—304 sworn officers, 6 detention officers and 62 civilian personnel. Of the 304 sworn officers, 139 are patrol officers. According to Guam Public law, however, GPD should have approximately 464 patrol officers covering the precincts.

GFD employs 261 uniformed firefighters and 28 civilian personnel, totaling 289. The National Fire Protection Association requires that GFD have enough personnel and trucks to meet a 4-minute response time for first responders and an 8-minute response time to 90 percent of the incidents for advanced life support equipment arrival or full alarm response.

GHS has no requirement to hire a certain number of employees. It currently has 21 employees, 5 of which are detailed from GPD and GFD.

### Equipment

GPD operates 50 marked patrol vehicles, consisting of 31 patrol cars and 19 motorcycles. These patrol vehicles are subject to use 24 hours per day and 7 days a week.

GFD has 1 pumper truck at each of its 12 fire stations. It has seven ambulances— four of which it leases on a 1-year term. In addition, GFD is in the process of procuring three more ambulances using U.S. Department of the Interior, Office of Insular Affairs funds.

GHS operates a mobile communications vehicle, which is equipped with $1 million worth of communication technology equipment that GHS has on standby for emergencies and uses for outreach, training, and local events. It also owns four 4 x 4 vehicles for responses to emergencies and disasters, and two vans and two trucks for day-to-day operations.

### Infrastructure

GPD has four precincts, a building used for police headquarters, and a Forensic Crime Lab. GPD moved into the police headquarters as a temporary location in December 2011. GFD occupies 12 fire stations, with its headquarters located in a former storage facility. GHS is located primarily underground in Agana Heights.

### Budget

In fiscal year (FY) 2011, GPD received $23 million in funding plus approximately $6 million in available active Federal grants. GPD distributes about 93 percent of its general fund budget to personnel, including salary, benefits, and overtime. In FY 2011, GFD received $33.6 million in funding plus approximately $2.2 million in available active Federal grants. GFD distributes about 96 percent of its general fund budget to payroll. GHS receives 100 percent of its budget in Federal funding.

### Comparable Operations

We compared GPD and GFD operations to operations in Maui County, HI, because the islands share similar population size, similar geographic limitations, and an economy based on tourism. Maui County has a population of approximately 155,000, which is less than Guam, and includes the islands of Maui, Molokai, and Lanai. Despite a population difference of about 25,000, Maui County has more stations/precincts, uniformed/sworn personnel, and patrol vehicles or fire trucks than the island of Guam (see figure 1).

## Maui County's Fire and Police Departments versus Guam's Fire and Police Departments

| | Maui Fire Department | Guam Fire Department | Maui Police Department | Guam Police Department |
|---|---|---|---|---|
| Population | 155,000 | 180,000 | 155,000 | 180,000 |
| Stations/ Precincts | 14 | 12 | 6 | 4 |
| Substations/ Kobans | 0 | 0 | 9 | 6 |
| Total Personnel | 312 | 289 | 462 | 372 |
| Uniformed/Sworn Personnel | 299 | 261 | 344 | 304 |
| Emergency Apparatus (Fire Trucks) | 36 | 12 | N/A | N/A |
| Ambulances | 0 | 7 | N/A | N/A |
| Patrol Vehicles | N/A | N/A | 119 | 50 |
| Relief Vehicles (Y/N) | Yes | No | Yes | No |

Figure 1. Comparison of Maui's police and fire departments to Guam's police and fire departments.

# Findings

The Government of Guam (GovGuam) has a public safety program, but it is not well planned or funded. GPD and GFD are unable to meet the needs of the citizens of Guam or prepare for any increase in population. GHS currently is better prepared to meet the needs of Guam's citizens but receives 100 percent of its budget from Federal funds with no plan to cover the losses of a decreasing Federal revenue stream.

Further, Guam public safety entities do not have service-delivery metrics in place to compare service delivery to expectations. Without knowing what the needs, resources, and the level of citizen service expectations are, it is difficult to plan or budget for meeting those expectations.

## Personnel Challenges

While public law mandates Guam to meet a minimum amount of patrol officers for each GPD precinct, and GFD strives to follow U.S. National standards for staffing and equipment, the police and fire departments are unable to meet personnel standards. In addition, Guam has not determined if the current laws and standards that the public safety entities attempt to follow correspond to the level of service Guam's citizens desire.

### Guam Police Department

As of March 2012, GPD has 304 sworn police officers, which according to GPD leadership, is approximately 60 officers short from its current staffing needs. In addition, 53 of the sworn police officers are deployed to military duties. To compare, Maui County, HI Police Department, which serves a population 25,000 less than Guam, has 344 sworn personnel and can employ up to 375.

Of the 304 sworn GPD officers, 139 patrol officers cover 4 precincts. Each precinct has three to five officers per shift. According to Guam Public Law, each village must have a minimum of two police officers capable of patrol and responding to calls at all times, and one additional officer is required for each additional 2,000 residents for each shift. Therefore, by law GPD should have 464 patrol officers to cover the GPD precincts.

In addition, each precinct has approximately the same number of officers regardless of the population. For instance, the Dededo precinct has only four officers on duty per shift. Dededo, however, has the highest population, at approximately 74,000—25,000 higher than the next highest populated precinct. The precinct should have 171 officers but has only 37.

The increase in population following the buildup will exacerbate the staffing shortfall. According to "The Final Environmental Impact Statement"[1] (EIS) prepared by the U.S. Navy, GPD needs to hire an additional 117 officers for the buildup based on the projection of the number of U.S. Marines arriving. The estimate does not account for the addition of needed civilian support staff. GPD leadership estimates they need to hire approximately 200 officers to meet both the current needs and the needs of the buildup.

## Guam Fire Department

GFD does not have enough staff to meet Guam's current needs. GFD has 289 employees, 261 of which are uniformed firefighters. According to the Chief, the fire department is short about 100 firefighters. Comparatively, Maui's fire department has 312 employees, not including personnel for ambulance service. Of the 312 employees, 299 are uniformed firefighters.

The National Fire Protection Association requires that GFD have enough personnel and trucks to meet a 4-minute response time for first responders and an 8-minute response time to 90 percent of the incidents for advanced life support[2] equipment arrival or full alarm response.[3] In addition, the Association recommends five to six on-duty personnel per engine company.[4] According to the EIS, despite meeting response time requirements, GFD does not comply on a consistent basis with the recommended staffing ratio per engine company due to sick leave, vacations, and deployment.

GFD has worked toward hiring an additional 30 firefighters. GFD received money in FY 2011 to hire additional staff but could not complete the hiring process by the end of the fiscal year. GFD is attempting to hire the additional staff in FY 2012.

GFD also has not had stable leadership. Four acting chiefs came before the current Chief of the current administration, which began in January 2011. Unstable leadership hinders planning and execution of hiring or procuring needed items.

## Guam Homeland Security

GHS currently has 21 employees, 5 of which are detailed from GPD and GFD. GHS has three vacant positions it cannot fill because GovGuam instituted a hiring freeze. GovGuam, however, does not fund GHS. GHS leadership believes the hiring freeze should not apply to their agency. Because GHS cannot hire new

---

[1] The final Environmental Impact Statement created by the U.S. Navy and released in July 2010 was created to assess potential environmental effects associated with the proposed military activities.
[2] Advanced life support is emergency medical treatment beyond basic life support that provides for advanced airway management, intubation, advanced cardiac monitoring, defibrillation, establishment and maintenance of intravenous access, and drug therapy.
[3] A full alarm response is the personnel, equipment, and resources ordinarily dispatched upon notification of a structural fire.
[4] An engine company is a group of firefighters assigned to one fire engine to perform assigned tasks.

employees to fill the vacant positions, they have borrowed staff from already understaffed agencies.

## Vehicle Shortages and Antiquated Equipment

Guam consistently has issues with budgeting for vehicles. GPD and GFD cannot provide the level of service established in their laws and standards in part due to vehicle shortages and antiquated equipment. Instead of establishing metrics for expectations of service delivery and maintaining the resources necessary to meet those service expectations, GovGuam has waited until conditions are dire before acquiring needed resources.

### Guam Police Department

GPD does not have enough vehicles to fully equip all shifts and have vehicles in reserve for downtime. In addition, the two-way radio communications system, although currently useable, will soon become obsolete and need replacement.

As of April 18, 2011, GPD owned 50 patrol vehicles, which consists of 19 motorcycles and 31 patrol cars. Officers use the patrol cars 24 hours per day and 7 days a week. An internally generated needs assessment by GPD states that it will need 50 more patrol vehicles and 54 more motorcycles to address the current shortage and in anticipation of the buildup needs.

GPD does not have a reserve fleet to provide the vehicles breaks to extend their useful life. Other police departments, such as the Maui Police Department, commonly have a reserve fleet. GPD vehicles easily reach the 10,000-mile mark within 3 months, at which time the vehicle warranty ceases, leaving GPD to fund any repair and maintenance costs. According to a GPD official, GovGuam has tried to budget and reserve funds for maintenance, but GPD has not received such funding.

GPD's vehicle shortage is due, in part, to the weaknesses in its vehicle maintenance program. GPD does not keep an inventory or supply of vehicle component parts, and sometimes vehicles sit dormant for long periods while waiting for parts or funding for repairs. GPD fleet maintenance practices include taking parts from a retired vehicle and using it in another. This serves as only a temporary fix and using rundown parts increases the chances that the vehicle will breakdown. In addition, we were told that because it takes too long to fix vehicles while waiting for funding, officers have resorted to using their personal funds to fix vehicles.

Poor maintenance could put officers at risk. For instance, two vehicles in the Tamuning Precinct have defective vehicle sirens. GPD does not have money to replace them, so police officers drive these vehicles without audible sirens.

In addition, GPD's wireless communication radios are antiquated, and by 2014, replacement parts may not be readily available if needed. GPD estimates the radios would cost about $12 million to replace. Presently, it costs $400,000 per year to operate the radio system. GovGuam also never created a cost-share agreement for the communications towers. For example, GTA Teleguam, a telecommunications company, uses the towers, which was not a problem when it was a GovGuam agency; however, GTA is now a for-profit entity and GPD does not currently collect tower-use charges that could be a potential revenue source.

## Guam Fire Department

GFD does not have enough ambulances to service Guam and does not have any reserve vehicles in its fleet. In addition, GFD does not have a viable maintenance program to keep up with needed repairs.

GFD owns 15 ambulances, and of those, only 3 are in service. There is at least one documented occasion in which GFD had only one ambulance to service the entire island. Some ambulances have been out of service for more than 1 year. GFD leased four additional ambulances on a 1-year term and is in the process of purchasing three more vehicles using funds from the U.S. Department of the Interior, Office of Insular Affairs (OIA). GovGuam has rarely purchased vehicles for GFD and has mainly relied on Federal funding or vehicle donations from other Federal agencies such as the U.S. Department of Agriculture.

In 2005, Guam Office of Public Accountability (OPA) released a report regarding the emergency acquisition of three fire trucks. OPA stated: "Unless a consistent funding source is provided to GFD for the purchase of necessary emergency vehicles and equipment, GFD will continue to resort to emergency requests for these purchases." The situation has not improved. For instance, in September 2011, a teenager went into labor at her home, the first ambulance broke down on the way to the house, and the second ambulance took over an hour to get there; the baby died on the way to the hospital. GFD had to again resort to emergency funding to procure the four leased ambulances following the tragic death of the infant.

GFD owns 12 fire trucks, but none have ladders with high-rise capabilities to service hotels and other high-rise structures on the island. In addition, GFD has no reserve trucks in its fleet. Having no reserve trucks will require active trucks to be taken out of service for maintenance, thus reducing the number of trucks available.

GFD employs two mechanics but only one mechanic is available to perform major work. As a result, GFD has a large maintenance backlog. In addition, GFD cannot sustain a viable maintenance program due to the shortage of spare vehicles. Further, GFD does not have an accurate, integrated system to track vehicle maintenance. GFD plans to implement a vehicle maintenance plan by 2013. Any maintenance plan, however, will depend on funding availability. While writing this report, we received updated information that two technical assistance grants from the U.S. Department of the Interior, OIA, were awarded for the purchase of six ambulances: three arrived on Guam on July 19, 2012, and the other three are expected to arrive in October 2012. In addition to the six ambulances that OIA funded, GFD received $1.1 million in technical assistance grants for the purchase of a fire truck with a high-rise ladder, two medium rescue vehicles, and a single rigid inflatable rescue boat.

### Guam Homeland Security

Guam does not have an early warning system for a tsunami. GHS purchased an early warning system in 2006, but has not installed it due to litigation and protests.[5] The current operational readiness of the system is doubtful because of how long it has been stored. In addition, funding to install the system may no longer be available.

## Infrastructure Weaknesses

Guam does not have a well-planned public safety infrastructure. The absence of proper infrastructure may affect GPD's and GFD's ability to conduct operations and meet citizen needs.

### Guam Police Department

GPD does not have a permanent headquarters location. A new central police headquarters would enable a centralized integrated operations presence to provide critical services to the people of Guam. GPD's current headquarters is at a temporary location. Consequently, not all necessary headquarters personnel or operations are located in the same vicinity.

Although Guam law requires one police station in each village, there are only 4 precincts and 6 kobans, or substations, that cover the 19 official villages. Two of the precincts, Dededo and Agat, are new and used funding from the U.S. Department of Housing and Urban Development (HUD). The Hagatna and Tumon precincts are aging, have significant maintenance problems, and are not equipped with appropriate safety features.

### Guam Fire Department

GFD does not have a permanent headquarters location and is currently located in a former storage facility, displacing equipment previously stored there. The displaced equipment is stored at various firehouses. Some fire stations keep equipment in storage containers, but we also saw that some store equipment wherever possible, such as bathrooms. This practice creates problems with accountability and accessibility.

---

[5] The litigation and protests were due to a vendor that appealed the sole source bid on the early warning system.

# Training

GPD and GFD do not have master training plans. Public safety entities' staff members need proper training to maintain their skills, stay up-to-date with current issues, and meet the citizens' public safety needs.

### Guam Police Department

GPD requires new police officers to attend the police academy. It takes 6 to 8 months to train a police officer. GPD does not have a training plan. Police officers, however, must attend Incident Command System (ICS) / National Incident Management System (NIMS) training offered by GHS. Other training includes annual weapons qualification training, use of force, pepper spray, and batons. Some GPD precincts offer sporadic training depending on officer strengths and weaknesses and available funding. Training is difficult for GPD because of understaffing, so they have to pay officers overtime when someone is in training. To remedy this, GPD tries to bring trainers to the precinct so officers do not have to leave.

### Guam Fire Department

GFD requires all new employees to go through approximately 6 months of training. Employees enroll in the Fire Academy at Guam Community College, where they receive 3 months of in-classroom training. They then receive 3 months of on-the-job training. Employees must also pass the EMT basic certification course and must receive 48 hours of continuing education every 2 years in EMT basic certification skills.

While GFD does not have an annual training plan for all firefighters, the firehouse captains are responsible for ensuring that firefighters maintain their skills and receive the necessary in-house training.

### Guam Homeland Security

GHS's mission is to have more training in all hazards preparedness for Guam and all stakeholders. The U.S. Department of Homeland Security funds the training. GHS must perform four exercises each year to continue to receive Federal Department of Homeland Security grants under the Homeland Security Grant Program.

## Recommendation

1. Establish a methodology to develop a service delivery matrix which would include needs, resources, and citizen's service expectations for GPD and GFD.

## Planning, Budget, and Funding Shortfalls

In the past, Guam's public safety entities have created strategic plans. These entities, however, have not updated the plans or tracked progress. Guam's public safety entities have also conducted needs assessments to identify necessary resources associated with the military buildup. These assessments, however, may not be sufficient to identify progress, funding, or achievability of the projects.

Guam currently has no public safety master plan; it is in the process of creating such a plan, which was originally slated for completion in November 2011. The plan is still in the development process.

GovGuam also has budget and funding shortages. Prior reviews conducted by the Office of Inspector General have identified weaknesses in Guam's tax collection process. A November 2008 evaluation of Guam's tax collection activities estimated that at least $23.5 million of tax revenue is lost every year because of inefficiencies in the tax collection process. While we did not assess the progress of GovGuam's tax collection activities, we believe GovGuam could use these lost revenues to help address the needs identified with its public safety entities. Instead, it has become common practice in Guam to rely on Federal grants for improvements and any emergencies. Half of the GPD precincts and GFD fire stations were built using Federal funding. In addition, Federal agencies either donated or funded the purchase of many of the vehicles in GPD's and GFD's fleet. GHS receives 100 percent of its budget from Federal funds.

### Guam Police Department

Despite increases in population and expected increases from the military buildup, GPD has not had any significant increase in its operational budget. Its budget decreased in both FYs 2011 and 2012 from the FY 2010 level. GPD has conducted several needs assessments and plans but has been unable to follow through due to the inability to secure funds. Of the four police stations GPD currently has, two were built using HUD and the Community Development Block Grants funds because they are located in low-income housing neighborhoods.

### Guam Fire Department

GFD has worked to raise revenues beyond its budget, but has been unable to use these funds to its benefit. At the beginning of 2012, GFD reinstated an ambulance emergency transport fee of $195 and a non-emergency transport fee of $95. This fee has been in place for since 2007, but GFD just recently started enforcing it. The revenue generated from the ambulance transports, however, goes into GovGuam's general fund and not directly to GFD.

### Guam Homeland Security

GHS receives 100 percent of its budget from Federal funds. In FY 2012, they anticipate a 54 percent decrease in funding due to grant fund reductions. Without the addition of local funds, GHS will be unable to maintain the level of service it currently provides.

## Recommendations

2. Establish a continuous review process to determine if the goals of the service delivery matrix are being achieved.

3. Determine a method to provide public safety funding from local sources of revenue.

# Conclusion and Recommendations

## Conclusion

Guam's public safety entities do not currently meet the needs of Guam's citizens. GPD does not meet mandates regarding the number of police officers and police stations in each village, and GFD does not meet U.S. national fire standards. Both GPD and GFD cannot fully achieve their missions due to vehicle shortage and delayed maintenance. Without meeting established standards of service delivery for all public service functions, Guam's citizens may be at risk.

It may be necessary for Guam to reexamine the level of service the citizenry of Guam desires. Once the level of service is determined, it is imperative that GovGuam works to meet those expectations on a continual basis and provide the necessary resources to do so.

Guam does not have sufficient funding to provide the level of service required by Guam laws or Federal standards. GPD, GFD, and GHS identified areas of need regarding the military buildup but funding has not been identified to fulfill those needs. Instead of relying on Federal funding, which has become common practice in Guam, GovGuam needs to find other ways to secure funds for public safety entities such as improving the tax collection process and/or adjusting GovGuam's tax and fee revenue structure.

## Recommendation Summary

1. Establish a methodology to develop a service delivery matrix which would include needs, resources, and citizen's service expectations for GPD and GFD.

   GovGuam Response: GovGuam responded that they are working toward enacting a service delivery matrix and continuous review process. Executive Order 2012-10, "Relative to Creating the Governor's Performance Based Management System Executive Steering Committee" addresses the implementation of performance-based management systems, with the goal of improving customer satisfaction in all government services. The Guam Department of Administration leads eight agencies in the pilot program. While there currently are no public safety agencies participating, the Administration plans to implement performance-based budgeting governmentwide.

   Office of Inspector General Reply: We commend GovGuam for creating a performance-based management system pilot program to improve customer satisfaction in all areas. We request more information on how Executive Order 2012-10 will specifically address the recommendation to develop a service delivery matrix. We consider this recommendation unresolved and are requesting that OIA track GovGuam's progress in resolving this recommendation. We request that Guam provide OIA with additional information, which we identify in Appendix 5.

2. Establish a continuous review process to determine if the goals of the service delivery matrix are being achieved.

GovGuam Response: GovGuam responded that they are working toward enacting a service delivery matrix and continuous review process. Executive Order 2012-10, "Relative to Creating the Governor's Performance Based Management System Executive Steering Committee," addresses the implementation of performance-based management systems with the goal of improving customer satisfaction in all government services. The Guam Department of Administration leads eight agencies in the pilot program. While there currently are no public safety agencies participating, the Administration plans to implement performance-based budgeting governmentwide.

Office of Inspector General Reply: We commend GovGuam for creating a performance-based management system pilot program to improve customer satisfaction in all areas. We request more information on how the Executive Order 2012-10 will specifically address the recommendation to establish a continuous review process. We consider this recommendation unresolved and are requesting that OIA track GovGuam's progress in resolving this recommendation. We request that Guam provide OIA with additional information, which we identify in Appendix 5.

3. Determine a method to provide public safety funding from local sources of revenue.

GovGuam Response: GovGuam responded that they agree with the Office of Inspector General; it is time to reexamine the level of service the citizenry of Guam desires. Governmentwide spending cuts are planned to take effect before the next fiscal year with funds saved to be used to improve operations. In addition, the Administration facilitated GFD's implementation of a new ambulance billing system, enabling GFD to properly track and collect revenue for emergency medical services. GFD hopes the new local funds help toward more training, equipment, and staff for the department by efficiently collecting this new revenue.

Office of Inspector General Reply: We commend Guam for implementing the new ambulance billing system as well as planning to use funds from the Governmentwide spending cuts to improve operations. We are concerned, however, that the additional funds from the ambulance billing and the planned budget cuts may not provide sufficient funding to provide the level of service required or desired. We consider this recommendation unresolved and are requesting that OIA track GovGuam's progress in resolving this recommendation. We request that Guam provide OIA with additional information, which we identify in Appendix 5.

# Appendix I: Scope and Methodology

## Scope

We performed our evaluation in accordance with the Council of the Inspectors General on Integrity and Efficiency, "Quality Standards for Inspections." Our evaluation focused on Guam Police Department's, Guam Fire Department's and Guam Homeland Security's ability to meet the current and future needs of Guam. We also gathered information from Maui County, HI police and fire departments. We conducted our evaluation from October 2011 to February 2012. As part of our review, we relied on the work of several internally generated reports and assessments, as well as the Department of Defense's Environmental Impact Statement. We believe our work provides a reasonable basis for our conclusions and recommendations.

## Methodology

We interviewed GPD, GFD, and GHS officials and staff and officials from the Public Auditor's Office, military coordination officer, former GPD chief, and the public safety advisor. In addition, we completed the following—

- reviewed applicable laws, regulations, policies, and other criteria;
- reviewed information from the GPD, GFD, and GHS Web sites, publications, and reports;
- reviewed various studies, assessment reports, and financial information prepared by GPD, GFD, and GHS;
- interviewed an official from the Department of Defense;
- attended the Oceana Regional Response Team meeting and training, Public Safety meeting, and Mass Care Task Force meeting; and
- interviewed officials from the Maui Police Department and the Maui Fire Department.

# Appendix 2: Sites Visited or Contacted

**Guam Police Department**

**Island of Guam**

Police Department Headquarters

Guam Crime Lab

Hagatna Precinct

Dededo Precinct

Tumon-Tamuning Precinct

Agat Precinct

**Guam Fire Department**

**Island of Guam**

Fire Department Headquarters

Dededo Fire Station

Astumbo Fire Station

Tamuning Fire Station

Guam Public Works (GFD Vehicles)

**Guam Homeland Security**

**Island of Guam**

Guam Homeland Security Building

**U.S. Department of the Interior**

**Washington, DC**

Office of Insular Affairs

**Maui Public Safety**

**Maui, HI**

Maui Police Department Headquarters

Maui Fire Department Headquarters

# Appendix 3: Prior Office of Inspector General Report

November 2008, "Tax Collection Activities, Government of Guam, Revitalized Tax Collection and Enforcement Effort Needed."
Report No. P-EV-GUA-0002-2009

Guam Department of Revenue and Tax has inadequate funding and staff, an inability to hire and retain qualified tax enforcement officers, an ever-increasing workload, and a reliance on manual processes and outdated equipment. As a result, tax information is not processed timely, tax audits are not productive, no efforts are made to identify non-filers, tax liabilities are not collected in a fair and expeditious manner, and criminal prosecutions are almost non-existent. Although the total amount of tax losses associated with these problems cannot be determined, we estimate that at least $23.5 million is lost each year.

# Appendix 4: Governor of Guam Response

The Governor of Guam's response to our draft report follows on page 20.

EDDIE BAZA CALVO
Governor

RAY TENORIO
Lieutenant Governor

*Office of the Governor of Guam*

Kimberly Elmore
Assistant Inspector General for Audits, Inspections, and Evaluations
U.S. Department of the Interior
Office of Inspector General
Mail Stop 4428
1849 C Street, NW
Washington, DC 20240

RE: OIG Report No. HI-EV-GUA-0002-2011

August 10, 2012

*Hafa Adai* Ms. Elmore:

The U.S. Department of Interior Office of the Inspector General (OIG) released its Draft Report—Evaluation of Guam Public Safety Report No. HI-EV-GUA-0002-2011 to the Government of Guam on July 13, 2012. It recommends the Government of Guam develop and implement a service delivery matrix, establish a continuous review process to determine if the service delivery matrix goods are achieved, and identify public safety funding from local revenue sources. The Government of Guam is pursuing these recommendations.

Like many jurisdictions within the United States, the Government of Guam is faced with austere financial challenges where a shortage in manpower, operational safety vehicles, and safety gear is a familiar story. The Governor of Guam has been addressing the financial crisis while simultaneously striving to improve services since the onset of the Calvo-Tenorio Administration in January 2011. The Administration's goals and direction have remained consistent: fiscal responsibility, quality service, and efficient operations.

The Government of Guam is working toward enacting a service delivery matrix and continuous review process. Executive Order No. 2012-10 *Relative to creating the Governor's performance-based management system executive steering committee* was signed on July 19, 2012. This executive order addresses the implementation of performance-based management systems with the goal of improving customer satisfaction in all government services. The Department of Administration leads eight agencies in this pilot program and, while there currently are no public safety agencies participating, the Administration plans to implement performance-based budgeting government wide.

The report also recommends that the Government of Guam identify local funding sources for public safety needs. The Calvo-Tenorio Administration agrees with the OIG; it is time to reexamine the level of service the citizenry of Guam desires. Government-wide spending cuts are planned to take effect before the next fiscal year with funds saved to be used to improve operations. In addition, the Administration facilitated Guam Fire Department's (GFD) implementation of a new ambulance billing system, enabling the Department to properly track and collect revenue for emergency medical services. GFD hopes the new local funds will enable more training, equipment, and staff for the department by efficiently collecting this new revenue.

The OIG overlooks important factors in its findings that calls its results into question. The report indicates that its purpose is to examine Guam's ability to prepare for the impact of the upcoming military build-up. The OIG references the United States Navy's Environmental Impact Statement (EIS), finalized in September 2010, to determine GPD's need to hire an additional 117 officers. The Department of Defense has since made significant changes to its plan of action as the U.S. and Japanese national governments adjusted the realignment road map to move only 4,500-5,000 Marines to Guam,

Ricardo J. Bordallo Governor's Complex • Adelup, Guam 96910
Tel: (671) 472-8931/6 • Fax: (671) 477-4826 • www.governor.guam.gov

20

substantially lower than the initial 8,600. The new troops are expected to bring only 1,300 family members with them as opposed to the initial projection of 9,000 dependents. Therefore, the cited EIS is no longer an accurate gauge to determine the increased service expected of Guam's public safety agencies. Supplemental studies are expected to be released sometime in 2014 and a new record of decision is scheduled for release in 2015.

The OIG's research identifies unstable leadership at GFD. The Administration clarifies here that the OIG research was conducted during a governance transition period. Although several individuals were selected as acting chiefs, only Fire Chief Joey San Nicolas was officially appointed by the Governor and received legislative confirmation. GFD's established leadership alleviates this concern and has generated additional revenue, maintained ten working ambulances, six of which were provided in addition to a ladder truck, two medium rescue trucks and a rescue boat by the Department of Interior.

The OIG report highlights a shortage of manpower in the Guam Police Department (GPD) and GFD. GPD augments its police force with the Civilian Volunteer Police Reserve (CVPR) and the Community Assisted Police Effort (CAPE) volunteers. There are 205 individuals that supplement the service that GPD's sworn officers provide. Guam Public Law 31-211 enables the CVPR to be utilized as limited term appointees, reducing some of the strain placed on the workforce due to military deployments. GPD identified funding and is in the process of hiring twelve new Police Officers and GFD plans to hire at least fifteen new Fire Fighters by the end of 2012.

The findings indicate that GFD and GPD do not have master training plans. Guam Code Annotated Title 8 Chapter 5 Subsection 5.55 includes sworn GFD and GPD members as peace officers, for whom the Peace Officer Standards and Training (POST) Commission is actively crafting standards under which all peace officers will be accountable. GFD and GPD will be responsible for ensuring POST standards are attained in concert with a future POST Executive Director.

The Government of Guam understands that a point of comparison is a useful tool of analysis. While Guam and Maui County share a similar population size and economic driver, their respective variables drastically contrast: 8.9% of Maui County's population lives below the poverty line according to the U.S. Census Bureau versus 23% on Guam. The difference in the two economies is further evident when considering the U.S. Census Bureau determined the average per capita income in Maui County is $29,180 compared with Guam at approximately $15,000, roughly 50% less. The effect of Guam's economic situation on government revenue underscores its relative financial capability to provide services.

The Federal government's failure to meet its obligations under the Compact of Free Association (COFA) places an overwhelming financial burden on the Government of Guam. While the OIG identifies pressing issues and shortfalls of the public safety agencies, it inexplicably ignores a glaring reality of the draining effect COFA citizens have on Guam's finances that the OIG points out the very same public safety agencies are struggling to obtain.

United States Public Law 108-188 amends the COFA and appropriates $30,000,000, which is woefully inadequate for grants to *'aid in defraying costs incurred'* by jurisdictions impacted by COFA as a result of increased demands in education, health, social, and public safety services. Since the Compact was signed in 1986, and later amended in 2003, Guam has seen an influx of COFA citizens in its population. Roughly 94% of all COFA migrants reside in either Guam or Hawaii, with Guam housing the largest percentage according to the U.S. Department of Commerce, Economics and Statistics Administration, and U.S. Census Bureau report issued in 2008.[1]

---

[1] Guam has the highest number of COFA migrants of 18,305. Hawaii has the second highest number of COFA migrants at 12,215, distributed between five counties.

COFA citizens' adverse impact on Guam is evident in the substantial resources utilized by public safety agencies to serve COFA residents. The three protective service agencies expended a combined total of $38,561,263 out of local funding to protect COFA citizens between FY 2004 through FY 2011. It cost GFD $19,643,199.00 and GPD $18,831,812.00 to ensure the safety of COFA citizens over the past eight years according to a January 2012 Bureau of Statistics and Plans report to the Department of Interior. GFD spent $3,518,778 to serve COFA citizens in FY 2011, marking a 178% increase from FY 2004. GPD faced a similar unsustainable burden by shouldering $3,076,213 in FY 2011, or a 143% increase for police protective services for COFA citizens. The financial impact was absorbed by the local government, thereby diverting funds that these departments could have used to hire more personnel, as well as acquire and maintain equipment and vehicles. The failure to reimburse the Government of Guam for these costs has strained the general fund and made it difficult to meet all the needs of Guam's residents.

The strain COFA citizens place on Guam's resources is further illustrated by their population within the Department of Corrections (DOC) and the Department of Youth Affairs (DYA). While GFD and GPD are first responders, DOC and DYA manage the byproduct of the services GFD and GPD render. DOC saw a 15% growth in COFA migrant population in FY 2011 from the previous year. Moreover, DOC expended a total of $20,481,706 in local funding for the housing of COFA clients within the past two fiscal years (FY 2011 and FY 2010). DOC spent $98.00 per day per day to house an individual person, totaling $14,723,716 to house COFA clients in FY 2011. This is a 156% increase from the previous year.[2] Like DOC, DYA provided $2,108,766 in FY 2011 – a 257% increase from FY 2004 – to service COFA citizens.

The Bureau of Statistics and Plans calculates the un-reimbursed COFA cost for the past eight fiscal years to be at least $440.67 million. No government can sustain adequate services to any population with such an onerous financial burden placed upon it without adequate appropriations to defray the costs associated with such an obligation. It is crucial and long overdue to increase the current $30,000,000 appropriation, as jurisdictions impacted by COFA are exhausting resources and compromising services. The dramatic increase in cost illustrates the accelerated impact public safety agencies bear in order to respond to the demands placed on them by COFA. Given the economic constraints and demographics of Guam's community, it is clear that if this trend of the Federal government's gross underfunding for costs resulting from COFA citizens continues, the Government of Guam will remain confronted with mounting expenditures that will result in the same lack of service the OIG ironically illustrates in the draft report.

The Administration is aware of the risks that public safety agencies' shortfalls pose to the island community, including current and future servicemen. The Government of Guam is actively pursuing ideas to decrease government spending while maintaining and improving services. The Administration has devoted the first year of their term to the development of a comprehensive Public Safety Master Plan (PSMP), which is in its final draft stages. The PSMP's goal is to address each public safety agency's inadequacies, personnel issues, reduce if not eliminate overtime and budget concerns, and achieve mandates. The PSMP identifies cost-saving measures that, if implemented, would provide funds to maintain equipment, training, and replace gear. GFD and GPD must hire civilians for administrative and technical positions to appropriately assign sworn personnel to perform their intended role. The PSMP is the first step of many towards an overall improvement of performance that the Calvo-Tenorio Administration is pursuing. The PSMP is the Government of Guam's response that offers concrete solutions that will streamline public safety and improve inefficiencies within the agencies.

---

[2] For FY 2010, the Department of Corrections identified 873 intakes of citizens of the Freely Associated States (FAS) who were incarcerated a total of 58,755 client-days. For FY 2010, the Department of Corrections expended a total of $5,757,990 for the housing of FAS clients. Guam, Office of the Governor, Impact of the Compact of Free Association on Guam: FY 2004 through FY 2011, (Hagatna, 2012) 11.

In conclusion, the Government of Guam faces numerous issues but continues to operate and service the growing population despite shortfalls. The public safety agencies on Guam, specifically GFD, GPD and GHS, are prime examples of agencies in which shortfalls in government revenue have hindered progress and service quality. The OIG report and the Public Safety Master Plan are long-term and stable recommendations that will undeniably improve agencies' abilities to fulfill mandates, hire personnel, and maintain and procure much needed equipment. Although findings within the report have excluded major factors that affect the island's resources, the OIG has highlighted areas and goals to work towards. The Calvo-Tenorio Administration is committed to public safety and upholding its duty to the residents of Guam.

Sincerely,

RAY TENORIO
Acting Governor of Guam

# Appendix 5: Status of Recommendations

| Recommendation | Status | Action Required |
|:---:|:---:|:---|
| 1 | Unresolved | Provide OIA with additional information as to how Executive Order 2012-10 will specifically address the recommendation to develop a service delivery matrix. Include target dates for completion of a service delivery matrix for GPD and GFD, as well as a responsible official by November 15, 2012. |
| 2 | Unresolved | Provide OIA with additional information as to how Executive Order 2012-10 will specifically address the recommendation to establish a continuous review process. Include target dates for implementing a review process, as well as a responsible official by November 15, 2012. |
| 3 | Unresolved | Provide OIA with additional information on the level of funding that will be directed to the public safety agencies to improve operations by November 15, 2012. |

# Report Fraud, Waste, and Mismanagement

Fraud, waste, and mismanagement in government concern everyone: Office of Inspector General staff, Departmental employees, and the general public. We actively solicit allegations of any inefficient and wasteful practices, fraud, and mismanagement related to Departmental or Insular Area programs and operations. You can report allegations to us in several ways.

**By Mail:**      U.S. Department of the Interior
Office of Inspector General
Mail Stop 4428 MIB
1849 C Street, NW
Washington, D.C. 20240

**By Phone:**     24-Hour Toll Free          800-424-5081
Washington Metro Area      202-208-5300

**By Fax:**       703-487-5402

**By Internet:**  www.doioig.gov

www.ingramcontent.com/pod-product-compliance
Lightning Source LLC
Chambersburg PA
CBHW080942290526
45795CB00007BA/2863